Another City

Steve Coughlin

FUTURECYCLE PRESS
www.futurecycle.org

D1005316

Library of Congress Control Number: 2015933087

Published by FutureCycle Press
Lexington, Kentucky, USA

ISBN 978-1-938853-69-2

For Tamara

Contents

Helen's Barroom

My father explains how the woman whose mouth
slacks open in a coma, whose hospital bed rests
in the middle of our living room, was different
in 1967 while dancing at Helen's Barroom.
An old man, he forks the final remnants
of day-old crab rangoon and comments
upon a car driving too fast outside.
And this everyday observation is okay
because, more than anything, I need to drift

with that speeding car that fifty years ago
would have been driving intently
toward the town's only bar. The quiet woman
in the passenger's seat, so this first-date
story goes, wore a green dress
and the driver, hair buzzed into a flattop,
delighted in Patsy Cline on the radio.

The night must have promised a lifetime
of such nights: a hundred years
of that gravel barroom parking lot crunching
under the excited steps of brown shoes,
white heels. A beer-soaked wooden floor,
the world was Eddy Arnold
on the juke; her fingers promised
to flutter forever on her beer bottle
between songs. That young couple,
for those few hours, the envy
of each drunk shadow on a barstool—
and me now.

But my father, grown weary
of conversation, finishes his paper plate
of microwaved food and retreats
to the silence of his bedroom.

And my mother, with a machine pumping air
into her lungs, keeps drifting
further from us along with those nights
she still rode through town, windows down,
brown hair blowing, the darkness ahead of them
lost in neon glow.

Bing Crosby Sings the Blues

Long gone, those nights, my father on the couch after work. He'd dangle
his winter boots over the side—ignoring my mother as she ignored him—

and, for twenty minutes, listen to songs in the dark. Not father-son time,
not *All in the Family* time, not a shot-of-whiskey-before-taking-a-walk time,

it was simply the soft swing of jazz, the prairie twang
of Buck Owens. And at least once a week, as my mother cooked dinner

in the kitchen, my father played *Bing Crosby Sings the Blues:*
the album cover dark as a Memphis nightclub, Crosby donning a blue fedora,

his lips wrapped tight around a brown pipe. Twenty-five years later
and no record store can find it. Still the album plays in the living room

of my memory like the month of December,
which never seemed to end—an unyielding blizzard of white blowing

even in the summer. I'd shovel three inches of snow from the driveway
while my mother sat in the kitchen chilled by lonely drafts

cold as the Bering Strait. Unlike the other albums, it was Crosby's polished voice
that offered dignity to the silence of my parents' marriage. It was his blues,

and his blues only, that harmonized with the frustration of their failed love;
his sad warmth expressed the months they went without touching,

the years they buried themselves under separate heaps of blankets.
And now it's gone, not a trace among my father's albums as proof

that Bing Crosby sang their winter storm. But it happened.
Even without evidence, it wanders in the past: my mother in the kitchen

secretly listening—not wanting my father to know—to "St. Louis Blues"
("That woman's got a heart like a rock in the sea"), finding a bit of company

during the sadness of her days; me, trapped in that giant snow globe,
comforted by the Floridian breeze of Crosby's voice, the icicles melting,

if only briefly, in our front yard; and my father, tired man,
alone in the living room, boots forever dangling, playing that album

week after week—"Five Long Years," "It's Raining
In My Heart"—his purple-blue lips, so often silent, singing right along.

1993

Year my sister sat in front of an oval mirror covering traces
of my mother's face in her own. Year of the pea-green winter jacket,
Pete Salinetti clotheslining me off my bicycle,
three houses left on my paper route, my cheekbone free-falling

to the pavement. The cat's body ached with tumors,
its stomach a concrete block of suffering. My father drank Riunite
and watched endless episodes of *Matlock*.

Eight years after my brother was murdered, his head cracked open
by a tire iron. Fourteen years after my brother rescued the cat
abandoned behind Little Peach, and still my mother waited
for her oldest son to return home—29 in 1993.

Year of cat shit in every hidden corner of the house.
My mother insisted we not touch
my brother's yellow lamp on the porch, a crack down its side,
terrified it would break.

Always my mother stranded in the house.
Always my mother, lungs clouded with nicotine, refusing to get out of bed.
My father backed out of the driveway each morning.
My sister, school over, drove with friends to Dairy Queen.

Day my mother, alone, cat laboring to breathe,
finally carried it out of the house in a brown box.
Afternoon the veterinarian stuck a six-inch needle into its back.

We ate takeout pizza for dinner, my mother silent
as the family failed to notice the cat's absence.

Morning I waited for the school bus on the sidewalk
still not aware
preferring cold morning air to the heated house.
Afternoon my sister stayed late for softball practice. Day my mother—
always in a blue bathrobe, always with a cigarette—
sat at the kitchen table even more alone than she was before.

Matlock

In those thin hours between jobs
my father indulged in his Matlock obsession.
Consistent as the family ignoring his presence,
weekday afternoons were dedicated to the sanctuary
of another syndicated episode of *Matlock,* lawyer extraordinaire,
defending clients lesser lawyers deemed guilty.
These were the years after my brother's murder
when my father's life had become its own hostile courtroom.
He'd arrive home from work—his lips so often moving—
as if searching for words to offer my mother's silence
that assaulted him with evidence: the dark maze
of my brother's schizophrenia
that my father never acknowledged,
the night my father refused to leave work to offer comfort
as doctors pumped from my brother's stomach
a small pile of half-dissolved pills.
But during that solitary hour my father's lips were still
as he watched the paternal lawyer with silver hair
uncover the real culprit: he'd make certain
the innocent gardener living in the pool house
behind the mansion did not suffer
for the billionaire's violent crime; nor the lonely trucker
who may have made some bad choices
but was certainly not the villain
who dumped a dying body by the train tracks.
Finally here was a man who never failed
to uncover the hidden glove or call forth
with his calm, confident voice a secret witness to testify
to a truth no one else wanted to consider.

Boy at Night

In the final hours of daylight he refuses to stop throwing his football against the chain-link fence. His arm aches from the relentless throwing and the fence rattles as if the boy could drive a football-size hole through it if he only threw hard enough.

But the boy will never throw hard enough.

His older brother, fourteen years older, has been dead two years. The boy tries not to sleep because in his dreams his brother wants to return home.

"Let me in," his brother calls from the street in front of the boy's white house. His brother knocks his cold fist against the boy's front door.

Three years after his brother died the boy's mother moved him into his brother's room. There's a record player covered in dust that the boy has never played. His brother's hockey stick still leans against the wall.

He will not open the closet filled with his brother's clothes.

The boy wants his arm to be strong enough to scare his dead brother away.

He keeps throwing the football against the fence because he wants to knock the fence over and run behind the neighbor's brown house. After he knocks the fence down the boy's mother will call his name but the boy will not come home.

Emphysema has sprouted like a weed in his mother's lungs.

She is fat and smokes all day. The boy's mother does not have the strength to protect him and his father, with circles under his eyes, works through the night.

The boy's mother did not help when he was six years old watching a basketball game on television: Larry Bird backed his defender down and the crowd cheered loud as he released a shot from the tips of his fingers that spun smoothly through the air. The brother was in a heavy rocking chair, the boy on the floor, but his mother never came running in, her face a storm of anger, after his brother rocked the chair down on his leg—the boy was screaming.

He has thrown so much his shoulder is strained. It hurts to lift a glass of water before bed.

In his dream the boy's brother wants his room back. He shakes the
locked bulkhead door. He stands in the backyard looking up at the boy's
second-story window.

There is no moon when the boy wakes.

He cannot see his brother's red baseball cap or the stuffed panda bear
his brother won at the fair the summer before his death.

The boy's shoulder aches but he refuses to ask his mother for help. Her body smells
of cigarettes; cancer reaches down her spine like an icicle.

The boy remembers his brother, alive, skating around the hockey rink.

Games started in the evening. He drank warm cocoa from a thermos. His mother,
arms raised high, cheered whenever his brother collided into an opponent.

A Small Sign

Still in a canyon of grief, my mother worked with a hand spade
in the backyard six weeks after my brother's death,
frantic for company. The house was loud
with silence; her closest friends visited less each afternoon
and my father, arguing a need for money, had disappeared
behind the grey fog of work.

My mother was digging up dirt for a tomato garden
she would never plant.

It makes sense that when the bird flew by a third time,
placing itself on the lowest branch of the only tree in our backyard,
she considered it a small sign: my mother was desperate

for another round of Scrabble with my brother,
his fingers delicately picking up the small wooden pieces,
counting off points for each letter; his forehead
without a trace of blue from the tire iron that cracked his skull.

In this way the bird's reappearance, its exact positioning
five feet from my mother, was filled with meaning—
the shifting of its head from side to side
like jagged movements in a flip-book
suggested to her the universe was not simply an ocean of darkness.

My mother held to it tight—on knees bruised with dirt
she stared at the bird, its grey feathers unremarkable, convinced
the void in its black eyes,
as if looking at nothing,
understood sorrow after all the other birds had moved on.

What the Doctor Did Not Know

Of the ride to his office.

My mother, too weak to cup her hands, vomiting onto the dashboard.

The doctor did not know of the paper towel I dragged across my mother's lips, afraid of the incriminating truth.

He did not know, even after declining my mother's request for another round of radiation, how this woman slouching in a wheel chair was less than seven days from a dark-tunnel coma. The purple blouse she wore was from Filene's, her white shoes, barely eight months old, purchased at Payless—the doctor was not aware of these.

He could not hear my mother calling for me in the terror-black of night, her body a hurricane of pain, legs dripping piss, to help my father heave her onto the commode.

The doctor was not present in 1985 when I was seven and a swarm of hornets hovered by our wooden fence. He never thought about the poison running thick through my veins as my mother carried me into the safety of the emergency room. The doctor then smelling of aftershave.

He did not sit next to me when I drove to Walgreens three weeks before my mother died to buy her a new makeup case and a small carton of milk.

I did not confide how each morning my mother, back flat on the faded blue couch, tried to cover the pale white of her skin. The doctor did not watch me tilt a mirror underneath my mother's chin as she lifted a small brush to paint her cheeks.

He did not consider how the white of his jacket was stitched with terrible honesty.

His rimmed glasses, his professional grey eyes, failed to observe my mother in 1957, a young girl swimming in a yellow bathing suit, my father five miles away, ten years from her life, riding a brown bicycle.

The doctor was not present for their first date.

He did not witness the silence that their marriage became. The doctor did not assist with the ten milliliters of morphine in the morning, the five milliliters of Ativan before bed.

There was a picture in his office of a green house. He wore brown shoes and tapped a blue pen on his desk, but there was no help, no gentle suggestion, when an hour before the appointment I tried to wash my mother's brown hair, its lingering stench of sweat.

There was no moment to discuss the desperate mess of dirty soap I abandoned on the rug.

We had pulled over by the side of the road, twenty minutes late for my mother's final appointment. The doctor did not know my father was in the backseat praying a slow Hail Mary. My mother, well beyond the protection of a seatbelt, could not stop shaking. It was winter and no one was in the car but us.

II

Rockland, 1995

Fly balls traveled with beautiful urgency. For entire afternoons
I tossed batting practice to Ryan LeBlanc whose drives to deep center echoed

with metallic authority through our empty high school stadium. The Red Sox
were still failures, seventy-six seasons without a title, but at various moments

that year everything made sense. Ace of Base rocked the radio
as I folded boxes in the dingy backroom of Themis Pizza

for a much needed twenty dollar bill. At the Hanover Mall Rene Ambrose
took off my baseball cap and placed it upon her perfectly combed brown hair.

We wandered from store to store sharing a soft pretzel dripping honey
mustard on the checkered tile floor. It didn't matter that Ryan's brother,

local amateur boxer, spent the summer in jail for assaulting a cop
in the Burger King parking lot because on his family's mantelpiece

was a Golden Gloves trophy that served as proof
not everything turns wrong. At The Candlepin bowling alley

a pin setting machine caught fire as Rene and I tied our swirling
red-brown bowling shoes. I still do not know what I meant

when I said, "At least we still have each other,"
but as we waited for the fire truck such words seemed to capture

an incredible truth even though a year later Rene started to date
high school pole vaulting sensation Tony McSherry.

Ryan passed his driver's test on the second try. We felt liberated
in his mother's Ford Escort, which coughed smoke every time

he shifted into third gear. In late September the girls varsity soccer team
formed a wonderfully long line at Dairy Queen. I imagined Rene wearing

blue soccer shorts, her flawless white legs with goose bumps
in the early autumn chill. Ryan drove to Reid's Pond so we could eat our sundaes

by dark water and listen to the Red Sox who trailed the entire season
by three in the ninth. Six months before the Rockland baseball stadium

would be bulldozed into a parking lot, two years before Ryan's brother
was shoved into a police car for selling drugs to minors,

we stared at the lights of our town off in the distance—unable to see
the Episcopalian church that had burned down in May

or the dark shadows of the abandoned shoe factory on Liberty—
seduced by the glow of each passing moment.

To Ralph Macchio

I do not begrudge you, Ralph Macchio,
for not answering the fan letter I wrote in 1986.
In many ways your anticipated reply—the tantalizing thought
of you signing your name on a letter addressed only to me—
was enough to lessen the burden of Mrs. Brown's weekly spelling quiz.
I might have been just another soccer player
assigned to Team B, but what separated me
from the other second-grade boys
as I stood on the front porch karate-chopping paper bags
was the idea of you in Hollywood
taking a few minutes to sit at a desk
similar to the wooden desk in my bedroom.
My letter to you was not completely different from the one
I wrote to Wynona Ryder when I was 17.
There might have been little hope for an actual response
but the thought of Wynona Ryder's elegant fingers
opening a letter sealed by my tongue
was enough to get me through several lonely nights
stocking shelves at Jo-Ann Fabric.
Today, between grocery store advertisements
and overdue student loan notices,
I seldom approach the mailbox with any thrill.
I even miss the anticipation of the secret notes
we passed in eighth-grade chemistry class—
the torn pieces of paper traveling
like chain reactions from hand to hand,
even though the only time I was the intended recipient
resulted in an awkward night at Sal's Pizza Shack
with the foreign exchange student who misunderstood
my sincere attempt to compliment her bright orange dress.
But then there was that girl in high school
(a senior while I was just a sophomore)
who I wrote a note to on yellow legal paper
asking her to the Winter Igloo semiformal.
Yes, there was the ever-growing weight of shame
as the days piled up with no response,

but there were also countless hours of wonderful anticipation—
while others ate unappealing squares
of grilled cheese, I imagined my potential new girlfriend
in a plaid skirt, her brown hair in a ponytail,
standing tip-toed in her red shoes,
a silver chain dangling from her pale neck,
attempting to slide through my locker's thin slit
a finely folded note of possibility.

Doogie's House

I watched each Thursday, 9:30,
the twisted rabbit ears barely capable
of capturing the distant signal of *Doogie Howser, M.D.*
This was the half-hour I hid in my bedroom
away from my mother sitting at the kitchen table,
blankly staring at the unwashed floor.

Doogie's parents—Katherine and David—might have quarreled
with Doogie over his purchasing a '57 Chevy convertible,
but in the end problems dissolved:
of course Doogie would return the very-red convertible
and make instead a thoughtful donation
to the Lackmore Institute for Childhood Leukemia Research.
And then there was Doogie's genius:
perfect SAT score at six, Princeton graduate at ten,
licensed physician by the age of fourteen.

Not that I identified with Doogie—who could?
But in each episode there was Vinnie Delpino,
Doogie's best friend, who—like me—struggled
to distinguish himself. And even if Vinnie's mother wasn't lost
in a black fog depression, both of us wanted to be included
in the annual Howser family camping getaway.
When Vinnie entered Doogie's house, I sensed his relief
at the living room's cleanliness: no lopsided pile
of newspapers, months old, no broken lamp,
no dinner-plate-sized wine stain on the dirty couch.

And then there were those invented episodes
of me taking Vinnie's place. Each afternoon
I walked from school imagining
I was headed toward the safety net of Doogie's house.
Even though Doogie had no interest in sports,
his father would still be my basketball coach—
it would be Mr. Howser who would insist

my ball-handling skills were better
than anyone else on the team.

It didn't matter if my own father, drunk,
walked angrily past my room. The door was locked,
and once again I had successfully contorted
the television's rabbit ears to produce
an only slightly blurry signal. Hours after the episode ended
it was Doogie's mother I heard
carrying the Howser family laundry down our hallway.
It was her dress that brushed against my door.

Song of the Hearse

Long black car of ornamental dignity, windows tinted dark, bumper reflecting
the cold morning sun. Car that silently passes through stop lights,

demands all other cars pause as it passes. Denise Arthur, sick girl, dead at 14,
driven to the cemetery while we offered a silent prayer

during fourth-period English. Car of summertime employment.
Dave Vetelino, his house next door to Magoun-Biggins Funeral Home,

polishing every distinguished inch, scrubbing clean each tire.
Mr. Magoun shaking my father's hand,

years earlier, asking for permission to move my dead brother's casket
from the viewing parlor. My mother looking down at her crumpled tissue

as the car's back door opens to receive her oldest son.
Car that promises decades of grieving, my mother praying to the Virgin Mary

to make the phone ring so she can escape the house's loneliness.
Dave backing it up each night into the garage, hanging the lone silver key

on a nail before walking home to drink a bottle of Gatorade. Car that forgets:
high school graduation and not the smallest pin on our blue gowns

as proof Denise's name was called during morning attendance. Rosanne Cash's
song to her father ("It was a black Cadillac

Like the one you used to drive"). William Carlos Williams insisting it be simple
as a farm wagon or no wagon at all—a dray dragged roughly on the ground.

Mr. Magoun, who probably never heard of William Carlos Williams,
insisting the car be inspected each week

for the slightest hint of rust. And Dave, three in the afternoon,
still holding the green hose because it's a job and this is his neighbor

and because Mr. Magoun will pay him twenty extra dollars if
he works until four. Car making possible the double quarter-pound cheeseburger

and large french fries for dinner, a pair of basketball sneakers from the mall.
Car that filled Dave's new Jeep with a tank of super unleaded gas. Dave's Jeep

now pulling into my driveway. His Jeep driving us to the ocean, the salt breeze
blowing, the tide rolling over warm sand. Dave's Jeep, its radio blaring,

its horn honking at the girls playing volleyball, assuring us like nothing else
that we'll never ride in that discreet and luxurious car.

Getting It Right

What could it hurt to rewrite my adolescence—
for instance, this time Anna arrives at my sixteenth birthday party

in a swimsuit. It wouldn't change the course of known events for me
to say we retired to the bedroom where I touched parts

of Anna's body that called to me like distant church bells.
The Globe can offer a retraction: due to an editorial error

my tennis-ball-crazed dog, Rambo, never collided with the fender
of that cruising Toyota. At nineteen, family eating dinner, let's say my father

no longer informs us he has throat cancer, there's no surgery that reduces
his voice to a whisper. And this time no one moves out: my brother lives

in the basement spinning a record twenty years long, an Eagles poster,
Live at the Garden, nailed above his bed; my sister spends eternity

in the bathroom perfecting the art of mascara.
Let Rambo catch the tennis ball at the corner of our driveway.

Let my father's voice call me to dinner. *The Herald*
can publish a new story: my parents purchase that '89 mini-van,

its tank big enough to hold thirty years of gasoline—hands on the wheel,
everyone buckled, my father leads us in song, "The Long Road Home,"

and Anna too sits in the back, her voice joining ours
as she reaches for me—her red bikini brighter than any brake light.

The El Camino

For my father polishing her each Sunday morning—
an Old Milwaukee in one hand, a yellow sponge in the other.
For him singing along with Sam Cooke crooning
from the tape deck. For Christina's pink and white miniskirt
and the way her skin looked smoother
than any Larry Bird jump shot.
For that Saturday night in September when my father dangled
the El Camino's keys before me,
demanding I repeat each of his instructions—
how the resentment I felt for my father,
who bestowed on that brown behemoth the affection
he denied my mother, disappeared. For each Circuit City
stockholder whose investments resulted in the construction
of an unlit parking lot. For the El Camino's six-foot bed
where my inexperienced fingers tore off
Christina's black bra buckle.
How we delighted in the El Camino's absorbent springs,
Christina calling my name
as if each letter had great significance.
For Sam Cooke filling the awkward silence of our ride home—
Christina not kissing me goodnight that night
or any night after. For my father, the next morning, discovering
Christina's torn bra buckle. I watched from the kitchen window
as he ceased his duet with Sam Cooke
and considered the small black clasp. For my father,
who I had learned to ignore
whenever he was home, tossing the evidence
to the wind and sidewalk. For my father dipping his yellow sponge
in a cracked bucket, rivulets of grime
dripping down its sides. For my father, nursing his last
Old Milwaukee, working into that Sunday afternoon,
re-cleaning each inch of the El Camino.

Did Not Speak

I wanted my brother to die,
or I wanted the wires stuck into his arms
to wrap around his twenty-one-year-old body
and never let go, the white hospital sheets
enough to finally make him good.

My father took me outside. We waited together
while my mother and sister stayed behind
in the hospital room. My brother had been unconscious
for a couple days. The doctors told us
to keep saying his name.

My father bought a Kit-Kat. He gave three wafers to me
and kept one for himself. He leaned against a concrete wall
while seagulls flew overhead. I know it was April,
I was seven, and I am almost certain
the sun was shining on my father's grey hair.

Before being led out of the room, I saw a white cloth
wrapped around my brother's head. I remember his body
was swollen. And there was a machine beside his bed.
I watched as it pumped air into my brother's chest.
Then took it back.

*

At seven I did not understand my brother's injuries. I knew nothing of
hematomas, of contusions, the brain swelling and pushing against bone.
I did not understand my trip to the hospital.

I knew nothing of drug deals gone wrong, of an unidentified assailant,
the force it takes to crack a skull.

I only knew my brother was the reason my mother stopped cooking family dinners,
why she refused to leave the house for days at a time. My brother was the reason
my father always worked and would not stop working.

I blamed him for most any bruise I suffered. He was the monster roaming our hallways at night, his footsteps always creaking, his hand about to turn the knob to my door.

My brother was the one looking through my second floor window. I could see the moon casting his shadow. I could hear him tapping against the glass.

*

My childhood has a thousand spaces. My thoughts return to the hospital—a seven-year-old son sharing a Kit-Kat with his dad. But I can't find the moment when my father kneels in the jeans he has been wearing for days and pulls me toward him.

When my father, his lips cold and dry in early April, kisses my forehead.

I know my father walked with me out of the hospital. He leaned against a concrete wall. And my father's lips were moving.

But no matter how I try, there isn't any sound. So I keep looking for something that means more than seagulls, April sunlight, a candy bar.

*

"We were young," my sister says. "You were *real* young."

I am a freshman in college and the two of us
have been comparing memories for the last couple hours.

"He had a moustache," my sister says.

"Dark brown," I say.

We discuss an Eagles poster above his bed.
I ask if he looked like our father.

"I'm not sure."

We can't remember any pictures our parents have saved
of him. We can't remember posing next to our brother
for a family photograph. For a few minutes we even consider
our parents might not have saved any pictures of us.

34

When I was nine, my parents moved me
into my dead brother's room. At night I slept
in the same bed one morning my brother rose from
and never returned to.

I lived among his belongings:

    a Marlboro trash can; a stuffed panda bear
    won at a carnival; a record player
    with a stack of records beside it—
    AC/DC and Black Sabbath.

My mother told me not to touch anything,
so the room remained covered in dust.
I didn't even look at his journals
hidden in a drawer. I did not want to know
what they said. I was certain
my brother's words were still breathing.

Silence eating fast food for dinner, a Happy Meal
with a small *Star Wars* toy. Silence sent to school
each day in unwashed clothes. A letter from the principal
requesting my mother wash her children's greasy hair.
My father waking at four in the morning.
My father driving to his first job
without the radio working, without the heater working.
The television screaming in the hours
before bed. The basement where my brother
smoked pot. My father driving to his second job
in a rattling car. My mother in her bedroom,
her head resting on a dirty pillow case,
her face, without expression, lost in the silence of sleep.

*

"There was a fire," I say.

"Yes," my sister says.

I am twenty-four. We have been comparing memories
for over six years.

"In the kitchen?" I ask.

"His cigarette caught in the trash," my sister says,
"but it was small."

I ask if our father put it out.

"I can't remember."

I ask if she remembers our brother stealing
quarters and dimes from our parents' dirty clothes.
If she remembers our brother's friends,
how they never had names, how their hair
was always long, their eyes heavy-lidded,
how their grins set off car alarms.

I ask if our father ever threatened him, if our father
ever changed the locks during one of those weeks
our brother disappeared.

"I remember Mom crying," my sister says.

*

I wanted my father to be a hero.
I wanted him to make sure my brother would never rise
from his hospital bed. I wanted my father
to kiss my forehead, to convince my mother to cook again.

I wanted him to make sure
no one would tap against my window.

*

Whenever my father was home, during those hours between jobs, I would follow him. I would watch him eat reheated pasta at the table. I would watch the reflection in the mirror of my father's upturned face as he shaved stubble from his neck. I would watch him watch television.

And always he was talking to himself. At the kitchen table, in the backyard while struggling to start the lawnmower, even when walking out the porch door.

My father's lips were moving; there were things he could not stop thinking.

Things that needed to be said.

*

"I'm not sure," I say.

"About what?" my sister asks.

My sister has been married for two years.
We're sitting in the living room of her newly purchased house.

"The rocking chair," I say.

"What rocking chair?"

"The one in the den," I say. "My leg was underneath."

"I don't think so," she says.

"He rocked down."

"No," my sister says.

"He wanted to hurt me. I'm sure I screamed."

"It's something I'd remember," she says.

"Dad was working, and Mom kept saying it didn't happen."

"I don't know," my sister says.

"But I see it," I say. "I really do."

*

When I was fifteen, my father started to come into my room
when he had trouble falling asleep. He would lie next to me
in my dead brother's twin bed. The two of us
did not speak. We would close our eyes and rest.
Our shoulders and legs touched, and I could feel my father breathe.
We stayed like this for hours,
never sleeping. The bed not big enough for either of us to move.

*

Still this memory I keep returning to. The one whose details I am never
certain of. How many different ways can I approach the day my brother died?

My father walked out of the hospital. He wore a windbreaker, or maybe a denim
jacket. I think there were seagulls above us.

I know my father slept next to me. I know he ate reheated pasta.

But I still don't know what he was saying.

Not while he tried to start the lawnmower, not while he shaved stubble
from his neck, not even while I secretly wished for the death of his oldest son.

*

"I was in the backseat," I say.

I am talking with my sister on the phone. I am thirty-four years old
and have moved a thousand miles away from home.

"But he didn't even have a license," my sister says.

"Dad insisted," I say. "They switched seats.
Dad wanted him to drive the last mile home."

"And he drove into the porch?"

"He drove through it."

"Are you sure?" my sister asks.

"We almost made it to the backyard."

"Where was I? Where was Mom?"

"I wasn't buckled," I say.

"We were never buckled."

"I remember picking up speed in the driveway."

"I don't know," my sister says.

"It happened. And there wasn't any sound.
None of us screamed. Dad didn't even say,
'Slow down.'"

*

Silence driving to the hospital. My family walking
disinfected halls, following brown arrows
to a silent intensive care. My father drinking
a cup of cold coffee. My brother's head wrapped
in a white cloth. A tube pushed down my brother's throat.
My mother beside his swollen body. The long hours
before my brother's death. His chest rising
as a machine pumped silent air.

*

The wind was blowing. An early April sun was shining
on my father's grey hair. I ate three wafers
of a Kit-Kat while my father chewed reheated pasta.
I ate a Kit-Kat while my father climbed
into my dead brother's bed. There was a fire
in the kitchen. His records covered in dust on the floor.
I wanted my brother to die as he stole
quarters and dimes from my parents' dirty clothes.

He tapped against my window.

*

And through these memories my father's lips move even though my sister says my brother never rocked down on my leg, that he never drove a car through our porch.

My father's lips move even though my mother sent me to school in unwashed clothes. I can see my father's lips as he holds a glass of water, as he rises to go to work at four in the morning.

My father's lips move as he leans against a concrete wall—his youngest son eats three wafers of a candy bar, his oldest son hours from death. They move each day I wake in my bedroom a thousand miles from home. They'll never stop.

Things I Could Never Tell My Father

You'll be dead within ten years.

The decades you spent exercising, running forty miles a week even during the coldest January freeze, hasn't kept you from growing old, didn't stop you from having a stroke while eating a dinner of liver and onions at Butterfields.

The day I turned 21, there was no way I was driving with you after lunch past all of Rockland's abandoned storefronts to down a few shots of bourbon at the bar.

When I was a child, I prayed each night you would not come home from work.

The sound of your car pulling into the driveway was my least favorite sound.

The sound of your boots on the front porch—those angry stomps to shake off the frozen snow—was my second least favorite sound.

Your dead wife and dead son are not waiting for you in heaven.

When you die, there is only the silence you've been practicing all your life.
The same silence I inherited that keeps me returning to your house each summer, waiting for words neither of us will speak.

I would have hated you as a young man. I would have called the police if I had witnessed you with a group of friends degrading men in front of their girlfriends by pinning them on the ground and removing their clothes.

When I was home this past August, I was sickened by the open wounds on your chest from skin cancer, the watery pus seeping through your shirt.

I would rather grow old in an empty apartment than have a marriage like yours.

I would rather never have children than wake each morning hours before the ice-cold sunrise—work so late everyone in the house had returned to bed by the time you cracked open a beer on the couch.

I know you have grown tired—tired of me still waiting for you to be a father.

I don't ever want you to leave me.

III

Haunted

Each night I wander the city unable to stop thinking of the quarter ounce of weed I never sold your brother—the night I broke his skull instead. I think of the gold watch that slipped easily from his wrist. Past empty car lots, the abandoned shoe factory, each night the same as that cold April evening. I still wear my frayed denim jacket, its collar raised around my neck. Past that same chain-link fence for 29 years, the green dumpster overflowing with trash. The frozen sleet begins at nine o'clock, my feet wet and aching. You have turned my hair grey, have made my back hunch with age, but never is there sleep, never do you allow me to drink a cup of coffee in the morning. Just this walking with the same tire iron hidden in my jacket. My stomach clenches when I pass the police station. Here is the diner I ate at an hour before your brother's death. Hands in my pockets, eyes on the sidewalk, I can't stop moving. Past the rundown house I grew up in. My parents are dead— but when you make me look through the living room window, there's the pyramid of beer cans my father left on the floor, the top one filled with cigarettes and spit. The black-and-white television blares. The city bus waits by the curb, but you never allow me to take a seat, never let my hands grow warm. As I wander past the industrial park, not a single streetlight turns on. Here are the rusted railroad tracks I can't stop following, my feet shuffling from wooden tie to wooden tie. Ahead the familiar grove of trees, an unlit bridge. Each night I glimpse the same shadow of a body on the ground. You make my hands shake—as I move closer, my chest begins to heave. I can't stop thinking of your brother's brain hemorrhaging blood. You make me watch as his forehead turns purple, his body begins to spasm. Each night you lean me forward, bend me like a doll, to watch your brother's legs kick out again and again.

The Invented City

Morning traffic is noticeably lighter—
the coffee in my super-sized mug never cools.
When I pick my father up at the city airport
(where the head attendant *pays me* fifteen dollars
for each half-hour my car resides in the parking garage),
my father's voice has returned;
as we ride past the numerous skyscrapers
under an eternally bright sky,
my father once more sings "Mack the Knife"
in his smooth baritone; but in the awkward silence that follows,
when we have nothing else to say,
I begin to remember his back is covered with cancerous growths,
that the bandage on his neck
is soaked with pus and blood.

In the city I invent, my apartment offers
an appealing view of the statehouse's golden dome,
of the cobblestone street below;
each time I ride the subway, a freshly ironed copy
of *The Daily Gazette* rests on my seat—
by the emergency exit, a napping cot
with clean sheets waits for me;
but no matter how I strain, I cannot imagine
my brother as a kind man. As I ride the blue line
to the Museum of Essential Art
with its permanent exhibit of Vermeer's collected paintings,
I still think of his cold face
as the train speeds past a block of abandoned warehouses.

Even my mother—who is young again,
who sits with me in a crowded restaurant
in the recently renovated waterfront district
and wears the same purple sweater she bought
at TJ Max when I was ten—

even as she flips her hair from her shoulders
while Eddy Arnold plays on the radio
and takes another sip
from her steaming bowl of seafood chowder—
I still cannot forget she is dead.

A Job in California

I've been told that there's a job in California.
A job for someone with a history of a poor work ethic.
For someone who's walked out of previous jobs without notice
    at least a half-dozen times.
One with four-month vacations, five-day weekends, and excellent health benefits.

Nora's by the counter refilling our glasses and I'm going on about this job
    in Sonoma looking for someone who wants to do nothing but drink
    Sauvignon Blanc for eight hours a day. "Sure," she says, not buying a word
    of it. And when I tell her about the incredible opportunities for advancement,
    that within six months I could possibly become Case Manager of the whole
    Sauvignon Blanc division, she doesn't even respond.

But this is a job with a three-hour lunch.
Where women come and sit by your side in the vineyards.
Where those same women inch up their dresses and let you look at their legs.
It's a job for someone who's willing to sell cheap Mexican imports
    from a wooden shack in Mendota.
Where country music strikes like a rattlesnake from a small radio beside
    the register as fat truckers wearing overalls come in to buy Carlos Toraño
    cigars and walk out with Hank Williams in their veins.

Billy leans toward the campfire and spits his whiskey into the flame.
    "Tomorrow," he says, "we'll ride past Furnace Creek, over Funeral
    Mountain, and 'cross them canyons. And we'll make it," he says,
    as frozen rain beats against his leathery face—"we'll make it outta
    Devil's Hole by sundown."

It's a job just outside of Tahoe.
One that requires its employees to spend their summers at a nudist resort
    at Laguna Beach.
Where Franz, the Resort Manager, makes the observation that it's okay
    to be naked, that it's okay too to wear clothes, but that it's not okay for
    a man's private parts to be sticking *out* of his clothes.

"Fine," Nora says, "let's just say this job's for real. You still don't know anything
about it. What's the money like? Do you have any idea where you're going
to stay? Really," she says, "it's not like California is right down the street."

But this is a job with winters that kill.
Where men disappear for weeks, even months, only to return with beards
thick and wild.
Where an infant sucks milk from its mother's breast as the wagon they're riding
in moves slowly along the Santa Fe Trail.

"Christ," Billy yells, riding his horse hard against the wind, "Jesus God-damned
Christ." And now the sound of gunfire splits the sky as a group of riders appear
on the distant plain. "Keep pushin'," Billy urges, as his horse kicks up a long
plume of dust—"And pay them sons-a-bitches no mind."

It's a job for someone who's willing to pan for gold in the Sacramento Valley
and listen to a one-legged man with a scar across his cheek pluck
"Oh! Susanna" on a banjo.
Where nights are spent drinking whiskey in the Flapjack Saloon.
Where the local undertaker has a handle-bar mustache and poses next to
an upright coffin for a picture with a gunslinger who has thirty-seven
holes in his body.

"This is getting ridiculous," Nora says, getting up from the table. She's walking
around the kitchen slamming everything—the cabinet, the door, she even
slams the window shut. "I don't get it," she says, stopping for a moment,
"things aren't any different there. Where are you going with this?
What do you think you're going to find in California?"

As light continues to fade, dark pockets cover the valley floor. Puffing his
cigar down to its butt, Billy flicks it over the cliff. "They're climbing that
ridge below," he says—"It's best we get movin'." In the sky a vulture circles
as it glides on the howling wind. After leading his horse through the pass,
Billy begins to ride toward the burning sun setting before him and spreading
like blood across the Western horizon.

Song to Mother Nature

I praise the bitter richness of your Ethiopian coffee bean
and each avocado grown with tender care
throughout the southern counties of California's Central Coast.
I praise the softness of your summer sunrise
even if most mornings I burrow under my pillow
to avoid the slightest suggestion of light.
Oh, I love your American West!
That July afternoon I drove through the Painted Desert,
appreciating spectacular vistas
of your pink-and-yellow mountains
made even better with John Hiatt's "Cry Love" on the radio.
And who could deny the arrival of springtime, rediscovering T-shirts
buried in my closet, even if sometimes the hefty scent
of your blooming May flowers reminds me
of the bouquets placed around my brother's casket?
Truthfully, I prefer you in my imagination. It was the idea, after all,
of your Jurassic age that decorated my childhood.
The hand-drawn pictures of Tyrannosaurus Rex covering my bedroom,
his compassionate grin, a Red Sox cap on his oversized head.
And how many times did I ride the half-mile wooded trail after school
through Island Grove imagining Renee Ambrose
on her yellow bicycle beside me?
I keep thinking of Winslow Homer's *Fog Warning*
hanging at Boston's Museum of Fine Arts—a solitary fisherman
in a tiny dory awaiting the fierceness
of your winter storm. Honestly, Mother Nature,
it's so much easier to appreciate in a brushstroke
your austere indifference
than when I drove with Tamara that long dirt road beside the Lochsa River.
Fine: I was speeding.
But still it seemed nothing could save that deer from shattering
the windshield like a boulder.
Before the accident a glowing campfire burned
in my mind, us bundled in grey sweatshirts,

surrounded by the leafy splendor of you,
not Tamara covered in glass,
the deer's neck broken, lungs crushed.
Not another reminder of the inevitability
of your final gift,
its hopeless gaze before us,
and me too terrified to look.

Song of Escape

I celebrate the 972 miles that separate me from my father's house in Massachusetts.
And every hotel and vacation rental unit I pass each time I drive to visit him.

Instead of returning my grieving father's phone call who—four years after
my mother's death—still refuses to sit in her spot on the couch,

I want to float like a weightless balloon across the state of Ohio,
high above the bland nothingness of the Midwest,

to any of the elite hot spring resorts in northern California
that so respect their patrons' privacy there's not a single telephone in any

of the finely furnished luxury suites. Instead of thinking of the numerous
hours my father walks around the neighborhood avoiding all the rooms

that once contained his family, I want to celebrate the finely aged bottle
of Zinfandel placed before me atop a table of richly embroidered cloth.

And each afternoon I'd visit all three of the resort's exclusive espresso bars
to indulge in several extra-large, high-fat hazelnut macchiatos.

And each evening I'd disappear into the private library adorned with numerous
upholstered chairs to read from a safe, manageable distance the harsh realism

of any of Theodore Dreiser's major works. And even if my father discovered
where I was and mysteriously arrived in his black swimming trunks

and lowered his seventy-nine-year-old shoulders into the curative
hot spring water beside me, Gilbert, my full-time personal attendant,

would know to turn the radio dial from the station playing Dylan's *Street Legal*
to the Red Sox game. Instead of discussing the lack of nutrition

in my father's nightly dinner of peanut butter and crackers, we would listen
to David Ortiz launch a home run into the right-field bleachers.

And even if my father announced his intention to spend another few days
at this private resort, and through sheer good fortune he had reserved

the room next to mine, there would still be the double-bolted door
that my father could not unlock and thick walls to drown out

his blaring television and there would be state-of-the-art pillows inviting me
into the deepest sleep so far from my father pacing in the next room

that no matter how many times he called my name
I could not possibly be expected to hear.

Special Recognition

Driving the streets of Boston, I keep telling Nora this city hasn't earned our love.
I'm insisting Boston has not adequately considered how dollar bills would dance
     out of wallets, parade out of purses, if we were only hired
     to make weekly public appearances.

And even as Nora refuses to respond, I complain that economists have never
     fully researched how cities might flourish from our presence—how our love
     could renovate the dilapidated houses of Little Rock, our kisses rebuild
     the abandoned warehouses of Boise.
I'm suggesting Savannah would be more than willing to supply us
     with an antebellum mansion if we only allowed local residents
     to watch us slow dance each Sunday on the village green.
I want Nora to appreciate, as she cruises the radio dial, as she lights another
     Marlboro Menthol, how within days of our arrival Grand Forks
     would become the passion-pulsing-Paris of North Dakota.

Let economists write their books; they're simply men who have never been kissed
     by lips that burn everything they touch.
Let them go on cable TV to explain theories overlooking the obvious:
     whenever Nora's morning-grey eyes gaze upon me, whenever the tips
     of her fingers touch the yearning follicles on my neck, companies within
     a ten-mile radius rise twenty points on the stock exchange.

Nora needs to know, even as she covers her ears with her hands, that our kind
     of love deserves special recognition: a free hazelnut coffee or low-fat cranberry
     muffin from every Dunkin' Donuts in the greater Boston area.
Stopped at a downtown traffic light, I tell Nora it's time for Santa Fe to consider
     the mystery of *us,* for our love to be viewed by each inhabitant
     from the fiery peaks of the Sangre de Christo Mountains.

And even as Nora unbuckles her seatbelt, as she places her hand on the
     door handle, I insist she understand how any couple on any street in
     any other city in all of America would provide her and me with
     countless signed checks simply to watch us share a bowl of
     Cherry Garcia ice cream on the living room couch.

I'm saying the time has arrived, she needs to say yes. I'm begging Nora to stay
   in the car because, in only moments, I'm more than convinced, this feverish
   red light before us will turn, the break I've been waiting for,
   into an unstoppable, ATM-withdrawable, river-flowing green.

Adam's Thirst

How each day ends with silence.
Adam and Eve washing dishes, like us now. How she, like you,
wore size nine slippers. How he searched for words
to describe the way she scrubbed each spoon.
Tonight you're reading *National Geographic,*
and I find myself, like Adam,
without a definition for this thirst.

In the bathroom you brush your hair,
stroke after stroke, and I search for a phrase
that goes beyond burning-chestnut blonde.
How Eve, like you, walked light as a ghost.
How each night she ate seven cherries on the couch.
How Adam climbed into bed unable to explain
the softness of her exhalations.

How I watch you sleep. How in this darkness I lean over you,
as he did her when words were young,
to watch your shoulder rise, now fall.
And from the time when history was small enough for two,
Adam's voice reaches me:
"What is this," he asks. "What *is* this, God?"

Winter Refrain

Let's be honest, it snowed every day. 8:07 a.m., and you scraping ice
from your windshield, that thankless circle you stared through all winter

when the same flake touched your shoulder like a secret.
Each day you drove to work, wind from the west,

while she packed her lilac bathrobe and took *The Collected Poems
of W. B. Yeats.* That same sunset-purple Trans Am passed you

on the inside lane, and when you finally sat at your desk,
walls the color of rain, you listened, always, to "Sloop John B."

"Let me go home," you sang, "Let me go home." But each day

she took the bottle of late-harvest Riesling, that framed photograph
of Elvis with lamb-chop sideburns, every fire-browned brick in the fireplace.

During break you ate a tuna fish sandwich and carrot sticks while she took
the black table lamp you bought together at Pier One.

5:32 p.m., and you driving through eight inches of snow singing
"Hoist up the John B.'s sail, see how the main sail sets."

But each day the front door was gone from its frame,

the frame gone from your blue-shingled house. She had taken
that first date to Olive Garden, the Butter Pecan ice cream cone

you shared in Paragon Park. Let's be honest, it was a blizzard,
even if no one else noticed. And each night you walked the yard searching

for the kitchen, for her rain-cloud colored sneakers in the hallway.
There was nothing. Just your voice lost in furious snow.

Another Life

The man driving past our house, heater cranking in the winter blizzard,
is not my father. His hair buzzed into a flattop has not faded to pepper-grey.
There are no midnight-black circles under his eyes.

This man does not wear my father's old jacket heavy as frozen snow.

Unlike my father, if this man opened our front door, walked in upon
the chilled silence at the kitchen table, our faces would not turn from him
as if he were a villain.

Because this is only two weeks after my brother's death, the man who is my father
pulls his '78 Mercury, its frame rusting to nothing, into the gas station and grasps
the metal pump, its handle burning cold, preferring these extra minutes away
from his family.

He even decides after getting back in the car, turning the ignition, to drive around
for another hour, which is exactly what the man who is not my father—the one
I have constructed to live the only other life I can imagine for my father—
does every night.

This man still owns the blue convertible my father bought at eighteen, roof closed
in the arctic wind. Even though he is my father's age, fifty-two, this man wears
the clothes my father wore at twenty-one—white T-shirt, jeans, polished
black boots.

Because this man never met my mother when he was twenty-four, she does not sit
beside him in the passenger's seat, smoke from her cigarette rushing through
the window slit.

This man never denied my brother's schizophrenia. He never offered excuses
of overtime to avoid doctor's appointments, meetings with the school psychologist.

My mother does not resent him for offering little comfort as their oldest son
lay brain-dead in a hospital room.

In the cold darkness, the man who is my father enters a motel room, neon
streaming in. He watches hours of basketball, deciding that this night—if only
this night—he will not come home.

As my father drifts to sleep, television blaring, my sister does not sneak past him, like she does every other night, as if crossing dangerous ice to turn the volume down. She does not offer silence to every question my father asks.

But for my father there will be the next day when he must once again confront the weight of his family's needs, the overwhelming anger of my mother's complaints, my relentless questions about why he did not come home.

Unlike this other man who gets to keep driving grey streets day after day, snow falling in a raw and endless winter—but at least the heater cranks, and still the radio plays songs that this man loves.

And each time he passes a house with white shingles, driveway not shoveled, a broken front porch light, this man does not look through the window at the woman sitting with her children at the kitchen table, plates untouched. He has no need to wonder what it is they are waiting for.

Another Perfect Sunrise

Even if a daily sunrise occurs
in the remote sphere of God's Heavenly Kingdom,
the thousands of angels residing there
would not understand it in human terms.
Certainly another pink-orange dawn
again lighting their cloudless sky blue
would be different from that particular sunrise in North Conway
on the second Thursday of July in 1989
because my mother, who seldom got up
before eight, woke before any of us
and put on her dirty blue bathrobe,
much different from the whiteness of a heavenly robe,
and because she had to walk on the wet wooden deck
of the house we had rented
for the last seven summers
to sit in an uncomfortable wrought iron chair,
and because on that particular morning several clouds
obscured the sun from view. But what made it most different
was that this was only five years after
my brother's death; that when we started vacationing
in North Conway he was still alive
and he, rather than my mother,
would have been the one to get up in the lonely darkness.
She could not stop missing him,
and that is why my mother clung
to such absurd ideas as angels who somehow understand
human responses and can be persuaded
to briefly stop braiding each other's waist-length hair
to help lessen our perplexing grief
and why, as my mother looked upon the few threads of light
that suddenly split the clouds,
she sensed the presence of something
I have never sensed
and gripped the arms of her wrought iron chair so tight.

Sacred Heart

I miss riding with my father in his El Camino, praying a Hail Mary
whenever an ambulance sounded in the distance. I miss my mother

knocking on my door each Sunday morning insisting it was an insult
to Jesus Himself if I did not get out of bed. There was the white cassock I wore

as an altar boy. The Feast of the Ascension when Tom Carter, yawning wide,
dropped the thirty pound wooden cross. I miss Father Barry's horrified gasp.

Everyone was Irish-Catholic; everyone pretended not to know
each other's secrets: Mr. O'Shea, in a green blazer each Sunday, who walked out

on a wife and seven children to a start a new life
with a twenty-three-year-old florist. The girl sitting beside me

in eighth grade had hair so fiercely red I couldn't ignore the crude thoughts
intense as sun flares. I miss Sister O'Connor, eighty years old, blind in one eye,

explaining the function of each bead on the rosary as Ryan McGrath
drew stick figures engaged in sexual acts none of us quite understood.

I will never miss walking to school in ninth grade terrified the distant sky
judged my every thought, or kneeling before my bed praying obsessively,

working myself to tears—three Our Fathers for each person I knew
who had died. I still do not forgive Monsignor O'Neil for instructing me

to say the Act of Contrition as penance for kissing Sara Cook in the backyard
while her parents watched television. But there was the annual church bazaar

where my father, so often angry, ran a ping-pong shooting booth
looking foolishly kind in a torn felt hat. And in eleventh grade Father Hickey

called our house—my mother answering the black rotary telephone—
to ask if I'd come out of altar-boy-retirement to serve Sacred Heart's

centennial celebration. There was the red cardigan my mother bought,
her hair done proudly, and me ringing the chimes one final time

as Father Hickey raised the Holy Eucharist. I miss the familiarity
of the uncomfortable wooden pews, Father Kelly's sermons

that oversimplified all human behavior to right and wrong.
And when my mother was dying, Father Hickey—who I had not seen

in fifteen years, his back now hunched with age—
drove to my parents' house. There was the dignity of my mother's Last Rites.

How we formed a circle around her, my father's cheeks red with grief,
as Father Hickey recited the 23rd Psalm. I miss holding my mother's

still-living hand those minutes before her lungs stopped,
that long hour we waited for the undertaker as her forehead cooled,

and how in the empty silence beside my mother's body I allowed myself—
once again—to repeat every useless prayer she taught me as a boy.

The Anatomy of Birds

If ever God's heart was drowning
in fifty gallons of despair, I would mention
the anatomy of birds as a flashlight
to shine through His heavy grief.
Avian Pallium, I would say, and God,
even if lost in the agony of a thousand thunderstorms,
would remember the kindness
of this gentle bone, how it protects the *Cerebral Cortex*
like hands wrapped around
a small snowball.

God would remember, upon hearing *Anterior
Air Sacs,* how once He took the last embers
of creation to give each bird
a small breath. I would say *Synsacrum*
for the tender way God fused
their *Vertebrae.* I would point
toward a lone crane and whisper
Syrinx, for sparrows barely above
the sleeping trees, *Fovea.*

If ever an ocean of God's teardrops fell
like boulders from a grey-black sky
each of us should recite
bones found in the generous wings
of birds, *Alula* and *Scapula, Humerus*
and *Ulna.* We should repeat the names of each
tiny gland, *Uropygial, Malaclemys,*
our recitation not stopping
until God's swollen heart had risen
from its midnight of sorrow, until God could once more
hear His birds singing, so far in the distance,
even as they fly against His terrible wind.

Another City

In the other story of my brother's life
there will not be abandoned train tracks,
his shoulders fitted as if in a casket
between the rails.

The city where he had lived—its sidewalks
of trash and second-hand stores—
will no longer be the place
where my brother wanders
beyond street lamps for a dime bag of dope
only to be assaulted by the purple force
of a tire iron.

In another city waits the arthritis
that will haunt my brother's knees
at sixty. It's a cold city where wind
travels hard through the streets and his lungs
struggle from nicotine ache.

Above a twenty-four-hour
dry cleaner is a small apartment
where my brother, pepper-grey moustache,
watches television; his cigarette smoke
with each slow year
paints the ceiling yellow.

Evening after evening he wanders
this city—past a parking lot half-filled
with rusted cars, a motel whose few tenants
shoot heroin behind locked doors.
Here it is always December,
my brother one of several
grim men walking the sidewalk.

And because he has no money
and the drunks at the bar

seldom remember his name, my brother
dials my house at a blurry hour
on one of those curbside payphones
that has survived
well beyond its real end.

Tired, I will not consider
how good it is to hear his voice
or how fortunate I am
he wants to joke about the Red Sox'
last-place finish—his fingers grasping
the metal cord tight—but will only
feel bothered, pulled once again
from my welcomed rest
by the burden of his needs.

Acknowledgments

The poems in this volume first appeared in the following publications, sometimes in different versions:

2River: "1993," "A Small Sign"
Adirondack Review: "Bing Crosby Sings the Blues"
Connecticut Review: "Winter Refrain"
Crab Creek Review: "Things I Could Never Tell My Father"
Free Lunch: "Getting It Right"
Gettysburg Review: "Did Not Speak"
Green Mountains Review: "The Anatomy of Birds," "A Job in California"
Gulf Coast: "Boy at Night"
Michigan Quarterly Review: "Adam's Thirst"
MiPOesias: "Doogie's House"
Pleiades: "Helen's Barroom," "Special Recognition" (as "The Economics of Love"), "What the Doctor Did Not Know"
Poetry Fix: "Another Perfect Sunrise"
Rattle: "Another City," "Sacred Heart"
Seneca Review: "Another Life"
Sweet: "Song of Escape"
Tar River Poetry: "The El Camino," "Rockland, 1995"
Xanadu: "Matlock"

Thanks to Mike Coughlin, Mark Halliday, Jill Rosser, Joe Wilkins, Lucas Howell, Robert Wrigley, Lloyd Schwartz, Jon Rovner, Sean Prentiss, Kim Barnes, and Tamara Toomey.

Cover artwork, "Path and Destiny," by Premnath Thirumalaisamy (flickr.com/photos/premnath); author photo by Brian Kellett; cover and interior book design by Diane Kistner; Adobe Garamond Pro text and Adobe Jensen titling

About *FutureCycle Press*

FutureCycle Press is dedicated to publishing lasting English-language poetry books, chapbooks, and anthologies in both print-on-demand and ebook formats. Founded in 2007 by long-time independent editor/publishers and partners Diane Kistner and Robert S. King, the press incorporated as a nonprofit in 2012. A number of our editors are distinguished poets and writers in their own right, and we have been actively involved in the small press movement going back to the early seventies.

The FutureCycle Poetry Book Prize and honorarium is awarded annually for the best full-length volume of poetry we publish in a calendar year. Introduced in 2013, our Good Works projects are anthologies devoted to issues of universal significance, with all proceeds donated to a related worthy cause. Our Selected Poems series highlights contemporary poets with a substantial body of work to their credit; with this series we strive to resurrect work that has had limited distribution and is now out of print.

We are dedicated to giving all of the authors we publish the care their work deserves, making our catalog of titles the most diverse and distinguished it can be, and paying forward any earnings to fund more great books.

We've learned a few things about independent publishing over the years. We've also evolved a unique, resilient publishing model that allows us to focus mainly on vetting and preserving for posterity the most books of exceptional quality without becoming overwhelmed with bookkeeping and mailing, fundraising activities, or taxing editorial and production "bubbles." To find out more about what we are doing, come see us at www.futurecycle.org.

The FutureCycle Poetry Book Prize

All full-length volumes of poetry published by FutureCycle Press in a given calendar year are considered for the annual FutureCycle Poetry Book Prize. This allows us to consider each submission on its own merits, outside of the context of a contest. Too, the judges see the finished book, which will have benefitted from the beautiful book design and strong editorial gloss we are famous for.

The book ranked the best in judging is announced as the prize-winner in the subsequent year. There is no fixed monetary award; instead, the winning poet receives an honorarium of 20% of the total net royalties from all poetry books and chapbooks the press sold online in the year the winning book was published. The winner is also accorded the honor of being on the panel of judges for the next year's competition; all judges receive copies of all contending books to keep for their personal library.

CPSIA information can be obtained at www.ICGtesting.com
Printed in the USA
LVOW07s0052181115

463097LV00019B/144/P

9 781938 853692